# We're from
# Indonesia

Emma Lynch

Heinemann Library
Chicago, Illinois

Customer Service 888-454-2279
Visit our website at www.heinemannlibrary.com

Editorial: Jilly Attwood, Kate Bellamy, Adam Miller
Design: Ron Kamen and Celia Jones
Picture research: Maria Joannou, Erica Newbery
Photographer: Beth Evans
Production: Severine Ribierre

Originated by Ambassador Litho Ltd
Printed and bound in China by South China Printing Company Ltd

09 08 07 06 05
10 9 8 7 6 5 4 3 2 1

Library of Congress Cataloging-in-Publication Data
Lynch, Emma.
  We're from Indonesia / Emma Lynch.
    p. cm. -- (We're from)
  Includes bibliographical references and index.
  ISBN 1-4034-5804-9 (lib. bdg.) -- ISBN 1-4034-5813-8 (pbk.)  1.  Indonesia--Social life and customs--Juvenile literature. 2.  Children--Indonesia--Juvenile literature. 3.  Family--Indonesia--Juvenile literature.  I. Title. II. Series.
  DS610.L96 2005
  959.804--dc22

                              2005002615

Acknowledgements
The publishers would like to thank the following for permission to reproduce photographs:
Harcourt Education pp. 4, 5a, 5b, 6, 7a, 7b, 8a, 8b, 9, 10a, 10b, 11, 12a, 12b, 13a, 13b, 14a, 14b, 15a, 15b, 16a, 16b, 17a, 17b, 18a, 18b, 19a, 19b, 20, 21a, 21b, 22, 23a, 23b, 24, 25a, 25b, 26a, 26b, 27a, 27b, 28a, 28b, 29a, 29b, 30c (Beth Evans), 30a, 30c.

Cover photograph of school children from Indonesia reproduced with permission of Harcourt Education Ltd/Beth Evans.

Many thanks to Adline, Dihan, Nopppy, and their families.

# Contents

Some words are shown in bold, **like this**. You can find out what they mean by looking in the glossary.

# Where Is Indonesia?

To learn about Indonesia, we meet three children who live there. Indonesia is a country in Asia. It is made up of lots of islands.

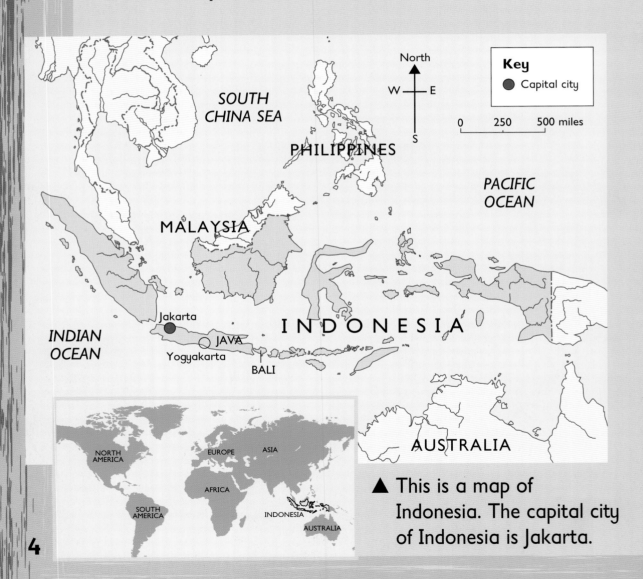

▲ This is a map of Indonesia. The capital city of Indonesia is Jakarta.

There are many small islands in Indonesia. Some of the larger islands have mountains and **volcanoes**. The weather in Indonesia is **tropical**.

# Meet Adlina

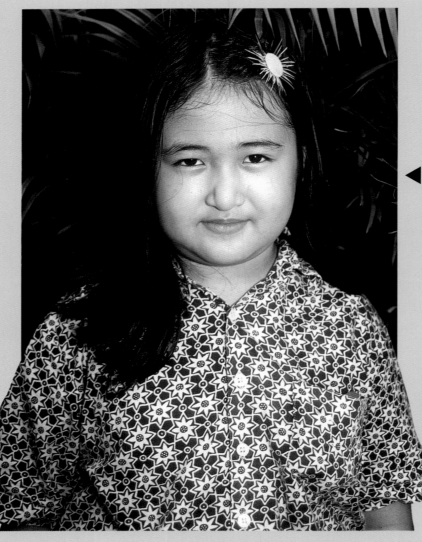

Adlina is seven years old. She lives in a small village near Jakarta on the island of Java. She lives with her mother, father, and sister.

◀ Adlina and her family are Muslims.

Adlina helps her parents around the house. She washes the dishes. She also cleans her bedroom and helps in the garden.

**Adlina's father**

**Adlina's mother**

**Adlina**

**Adlina's sister**

◀ Adlina's family live in a house made of bricks and **bamboo**.

# Adlina's School

Adlina goes to school five mornings a week. School starts at seven in the morning. Adlina walks to school with her best friend Kaina.

◀ Kaina lives next door to Adlina.

▲ This is Adlina's class.

Adlina enjoys school. She hopes to go to college one day. She studies Indonesian language and history, math, religion, science, English, and art.

# Playing

Adlina does not have any homework. After school she likes to play with her friends. She plays *dampu* with Kaina. *Dampu* is a bit like hopscotch.

▼ Adlina has a lot of friends at school to play with, too.

All the boys and girls at Adlina's school play soccer. After school they all play soccer together on the playground.

▲ Their coach talks to them before they go out to play soccer.

# Work in Indonesia

Many people in Indonesia work by making or growing things. Most of the work is done by people, not machines. People make bricks by hand, for example.

▼ Sand is gathered from the sea and rivers to make **cement**.

People also grow food, such as rice, to eat or to sell. What is made or grown can be sold to people in Indonesia or to other countries.

◀ Coconuts are picked for their fruit and their oil.

▼ Rice needs water and heat to grow well.

13

# Meet Dihan

Dihan is seven years old. He lives in a town called Yogyakarta on the island of Java. Dihan lives in a house with his mother, father, grandmother, and four uncles.

Dihan's mother

Dihan's father

Dihan's uncle

Dihan's grandmother

Dihan

▼ Dihan likes to pretend he is a *Tyrannosaurus rex* when he is eating!

Dihan's mother cooks. Everyone shares big plates of food. They use their fingers to eat. Dihan's favorite food is noodles.

# At School

Dihan goes to school six mornings a week. He enjoys school and does well at school. Dihan's parents buy him new books when he does really well at school.

◀ Dihan lives near his school, so he walks there.

Dihan uses an ▶
**abacus** to help
him with math.

Dihan has lessons in science, religion,
math, and art. He also learns
Indonesian and Javanese language
and history.

# Dihan's Afternoons

After school, Dihan helps at home. He cleans his room, the backyard, and the garden. Dihan likes to play outside or read with his friends.

◄ Dihan and his friends love playing soccer.

Dihan's father owns a workshop that prints T-shirts. Dihan has a job, too. He makes **origami** animals for his uncle to print in a newspaper.

Dihan gets paid ▶ for designing origami animals!

▼ Dihan likes watching his father work.

# Tourism

Many **tourists** visit Indonesia. Lots of people like to go to the island of Bali. It has **volcanoes**, sandy beaches, and **tropical** forests.

volcano

The Indian Ocean ▶ around Bali is warm.

Tourists enjoy walking up the volcanoes. They can also do water sports on the sea. Tourists like to visit the old **temple ruins** of Borobudur.

▼ The Borobudur temple is on the island of Java.

# Meet Noppy

Noppy is eight years old. She lives in a small village in Bali, near the sea. Noppy lives with her parents, sister, grandparents, aunt, and uncles.

Noppy's house ▶ is made of **bamboo**, stone, wood, and brick.

Noppy's mother

Noppy's sister

Noppy's father

Noppy

◀ Noppy's mother buys fruit from the market.

▼ Noppy likes eating fried rice with egg and chicken.

Noppy's family gets water from a **well** outside the house. They grow their own vegetables and keep pigs and chickens. The family sits on the floor to eat.

23

# Noppy at School

Noppy goes to school six mornings a week. At school they study Indonesian and Balinese language, math, **martial arts**, science, art, dancing, music, religion, and flower arranging.

◀ Noppy's class helps at school by sweeping the yard.

Noppy likes playing with her friend Sintya. They like singing and dancing and playing hide-and-seek. At school they play jumping games.

25

# Noppy's Life

Noppy's family and friends are **Hindus**. They pray three times a day at home or in a **temple**. Noppy wears a **traditional** Hindu dress when she prays. It is called a *kabaya*.

Noppy's family has ▶ a **shrine** at home.

◀ Noppy prays by their family's shrine.

▲ Noppy and her sister like to chase the hens around their yard!

Sometimes Noppy and her family visit the beach. Noppy likes to swim in the warm sea! Her family also goes to visit other relatives for a meal.

# Crafts

Indonesia is famous for its patterned cloth. It is called **batik**. Many women work in batik workshops. They draw pictures and patterns on cloth.

▲ A special wax pen is used to draw on the cloth.

Some beautiful pottery is made in Indonesia, too. The pottery is made from red clay. People buy pots to decorate their homes and gardens.

Many people work in ▶ pottery workshops.

# Indonesian Fact File

| Flag | Capital city | Money |
|------|-------------|-------|
| | Jakarta | Rupiah |

## Religion
• Most people in Indonesia are **Muslims**. There are some **Hindus** and Christians, too.

## Language
• Bahasa Indonesia is the official language of Indonesia. English and other Indonesian languages are also spoken.

### Try speaking Bashasa Indonesia!
Selamat pagi ................................. Good morning.
Apa kabar? .................................... How are you?
Terima kasih ................................. Thank you.

# Glossary

**abacus**  frame with rods and moving beads used to do math problems

**bamboo**  hard, hollow stem of a giant grass that can be used for building

**batik**  cloth decorated with designs drawn with wax

**cement**  paste that hardens and is used to stick bricks or stones together

**Hindu**  a follower of the Hindu religion

**martial arts**  fighting sport such as karate or tae kwon do

**Muslim**  someone whose religion is Islam

**origami**  folding paper into animal or flower shapes

**ruin**  remains of an old or destroyed building

**shrine**  place or object that people pray in front of

**temple**  where people go to pray

**tourist**  someone who is visiting on vacation

**traditional**  something thst has been going on for a very long time without changing

**tropical**  hot and muggy, with lots of rain

**volcano**  mountain that has a hole down into the Earth. Sometimes melted rock and ash erupt from it.

**well**  hole in the ground with water in

## More Books to Read

Cumming, David. *Indonesia*. London: Cherrytree Books, 2004.

Riehecky, Janet. *Indonesia*. Mankato, Minn.: Bridgestone Books, 2002.

Simpson, Judith. *Indonesia*. Broomall, Pebb.: Mason Crest Publishers, 2002.

# Index